QUAKERS
and the
Use
of
POWER

by

PAUL A. LACEY

Pendle Hill Pamphlet 241

About the Author/Born in Philadelphia in 1934, Paul A. Lacey joined Philadelphia Yearly Meeting in 1953, having first met Quakers through weekend workcamps. He has been active in civil liberties, civil rights, and East-West relations with various Quaker groups, but his professional field is a literary one, as evidenced by his book, *The Inner War: Forms and Themes in Recent American Poetry* (Fortress Press, 1972). Currently Bain-Swiggett Professor of English Literature at Earlham, he has also served as Provost and Acting President of the college and as Faculty Consultant on Teaching and Learning, and since 1979 has worked for Lilly Endowment, Inc., as Director of a program in Post-Doctoral Teaching Fellowships. He is married to Margaret Smith Lacey, and they have three children.

This essay began in celebration of Pendle Hill's fiftieth anniversary, a time in the life of the Quaker institution when it was appropriate to say, "look how far we have come," to assess our current position, and to take bearings in preparation for the future. To undertake such a process is to examine not only Pendle Hill but the principles which have created the Religious Society of Friends and shaped the institutions which give expression to what it believes.

Request for permission to quote or to translate should be addressed to Pendle Hill Publications, Wallingford, Pennsylvania 19086.

Copyright © by Pendle Hill
ISBN 0-87574-241-6

Library of Congress catalog card number 81-85558

Printed in the United States of America by
Sowers Printing Company, Lebanon, Pennsylvania

January 1982: 2,500

I

QUAKER PRINCIPLES are not merely of historic interest. What earliest Friends knew *experimentally*—that all human beings have within them the capacity to turn to, and learn from, Christ their Inward Teacher, and that the fruits of such learning are joy, peace and love in our inner lives and simplicity, equality, and harmony in the way we live with others—we may also know experimentally today.

To know experimentally means to know God directly, in the voice of the Inward Teacher, but it also means to know in the fellowship of other seekers, in the example and teaching of other people, which means, in part, to know through human institutions. Friends' experimental knowledge is woven into a number of institutional forms. These institutions are inspired by God, but they bear a human witness to the divine. And to the extent that they can express the Quaker principles in which they originated, they are "patterns and examples," in George Fox's words, for "answering that of God in everyone."

We live in a time when great numbers of people are profoundly alienated from all the political, educational and religious institutions which have greatest power over their lives. That sense of alienation is increasing and will continue to do so in the future. As a result, people are looking for alternatives to the organizations and structures which fail to meet their needs and for the supportive fellowship of community and the sense of efficacy which comes with being treated as persons.

Quaker institutions—our meetings, schools, colleges and committees—are among the "patterns and examples" which can point to more humane ways of living. But Quaker institutions are going through crises of leadership and governance like those affecting many other groups and institutions in the larger American society. We are experiencing difficulties in finding, developing and supporting leaders who can undertake the complicated responsibilities of leading us. At the heart of

Friends' crisis of leadership—a crisis which affects both the individuals in positions of responsibility and the institutions which Friends have created as expressions of our religious commitments—is a deep and unexamined ambivalence about the exercise of power. For we are fearful of having power and of using power, and we are utterly confused about the nature of authority and its relation to power.

Unless Friends can come to greater clarity about the nature of authority, our institutions, the instruments we have created to express our religious faith, will continue to lose vitality and purpose. They will cease to be significant alternatives to the dominant institutions of American society and will share their fate.

II

There are good reasons why we are alienated from our institutions. We are offended at having so much of our lives controlled by huge, anonymous bureaucracies which neither know our needs nor care to know them. We feel unconnected to, without influence on, the large corporations and government agencies which dominate our economy and our environment, which determine, with so little check on their actions, the possibilities of our children and grandchildren. Those whose power over us is decisive are anonymous, and therefore impossible to hold accountable, but we feel anonymous—nameless—as well. We are numbered, rather than named; we are data banks, not individuals. Virtually everything *about* us is on file, but no file-keeper knows us in ourselves.

But size alone is not the difficulty. For the primary aims of the organizations which have the greatest influence on our lives seem inimical to our humanity. Our encounters with such authority are catastrophic. If we are offended at the bureaucracy which administers food stamp or welfare programs which are wasteful and demeaning to recipients, what are we to think of a government whose solution to these difficulties is to eliminate such support altogether? If we are troubled by the heavy-hand-

4

edness of government regulation, what are we to say when our government sets out to reduce government interference in citizens' lives by destroying the protections of a Clean Air Act or Voting Rights Act? What are we to think when we see a congress wildly cheering the reinstatement of draft registration and the lifting of controls on agencies guilty of illegal spying on American citizens?

Nor are these the only reasons for feeling alienated. I once asked a group of my students, all of whom had been born in 1958 or later, to describe the political or social events they recalled during their lifetimes which seemed important to this society. The oldest could remember their parents' reactions to the death of John Kennedy; all of them could recall the assassinations of Martin Luther King and Robert Kennedy, and the 1968 Democratic Party Convention in Chicago. They experienced the Vietnam War as a dark cloud covering their early years; they recalled it as it appeared on the evening television news—inconclusive, endless, debilitating, enraging.

I then asked them to recall any political events which seemed to have given grounds for hope about this society. A few were vaguely aware of the Civil Rights Movement, the Voting Rights Act, the social legislation of the Great Society, and some gains in environment protection, but none of these things had made any great impact on their imaginations. Each was good, but none was a ground for hope. The events they recalled as exerting a positive sense of hope for them were one President's decision to withdraw from his re-election campaign and another's resignation. In short, what my students experienced as the two most hopeful events in America's recent political history were *falls from power.*

Many of us who are older have similar perceptions of American political life. Only a few years ago we were counseling young men about the draft, seeing some go to prison and others leave the country permanently. What were evidences of hope to us were likely to be acts of resistance to illegitimate authority, the triumphs of life in opposition: the "success" of a protest march on Washington or a rally involving thousands of people—but ignored by millions. In such conditions, respect for institutions or trust for people in authority will not flourish.

Robert Nisbet describes ours as a "twilight age," a "twilight of authority":

> Accompanying the decline of institutions and the decay of values in such ages is the cultivation of power that becomes increasingly military, or paramilitary, in shape. Such power exists in almost exact proportion to the decline of traditional social and moral authority.[1]

Nisbet claims we are witnessing two revolts, one against "the whole structure of wealth, privilege, and power that the contemporary state has come to represent"; the other against "the central values of the political community as we have known them for the better part of the past two centuries: freedom, rights, due process, privacy, and welfare." This revolt against established authorities and institutions, "the establishment," goes in two directions. One moves toward greater control, more authoritarian leadership of a people who have grown lax under a welfare state. For these people, the increased militarization of America is not just a necessary response to the threat of world communism, it is a healthy expression of discipline and militancy.

The second direction is represented by the anti-authoritarianism and libertarianism of what we have come to call "the counter-culture" or "alternative lifestyles." These "alternatives" embrace the widest variety of activities: intentional communities, communes, collectives, extended families, women's communities, simple-living, anti-technological groups, experimental schools. In each we see attempts to increase the sense of personal efficacy, to address the need for fellowship and the support of a community, and to struggle with the demands of equality and individuality within a community. New institutions and new patterns within institutions are emerging as responses to the failures of larger and established institutions—government, schools, churches, professions and economic structures.

Quaker-inspired groups have been among those most ready to explore such alternatives. Whom have these institutions attracted? Religious seekers, social and political activists, people for whom tradition alone is not enough justification for doing things, people who want to live experimental lives, who want to discover meaning in personal idiosyncratic terms.

The people I am describing, and the people I identify myself with most readily, are likely to assert that pluralistic approaches to truth must be respected. Such Friends are reluctant to say that something is the truth; they are more likely to offer it as the truth *for them,* the truth *as they have found it.* They are suspicious of appeals to authority to settle any question; truth, they believe, is a very personal thing. They do not want the institutions to which they belong to dictate beliefs to them, for that is to close off the search for truth which is so essential to our spiritual growth.

But many who are drawn to participate in our institutions, though genuinely seekers after wholeness, are also refugees so deeply wounded by the dominant institutions of American society that only what they are against has significance in their lives. Power itself, in any form, is the great evil they recognize; they are, for a time, rebels against all authority and all institutions.

We also draw people—most notably as students in our schools and colleges—who are longing for the support of community but not yet ready to bear the weight of responsibility which comes with membership in the community. They see community existing to provide their nurture—as it should—but they do not see that they must share in the nurture of others. Some are working their way through the trauma of broken family-life, and have been shunted from one custodial institution to another until they arrive at a Friends school or college. Some are the pampered offspring of affluent middle-class families taught to worship their own sensitivity and creativity, resentful of any check on their individuality. Their anti-authoritarianism, though it might be transformed into positive values in the future, is marred by what a former student of mine called ''class-induced impatience'' with the teachers and administrators whom they have been taught to treat as their incompetent servants.

But what I am describing does not simply involve the young people we serve. The wounded, the embittered, the deserted, the immature, the self-centered anti-authoritarian, who are also the seekers, are found at every age and in every part of Quaker institutions.

III

Though there is undoubtedly evidence for the cynical comment that ''organizations exist for the painless extinction of the ideas which gave them birth,''[2] we human beings, by our nature, have to create social forms to express ourselves and to serve the things we believe in. Some Quakers sentimentalize the early days of the Society of Friends as free of such bureaucratic constraints, but the Society very quickly developed an elaborate institutional network, a complex of committees and organizations drawing on sophisticated leadership skills for ''the communication of advice and help in solving practical problems''[3]—to keep a record of ''sufferings,'' to give legal and financial aid to those on trial or in prison, to oversee the good order of meetings and to recognize ministers, to keep the Society informed through minutes and epistles, to supervise publications, to wait on public officials and labor with them ''in the Truth.'' Quakers saw the development of such organizations as expressions of their testimony to the Truth, not as a falling away from pure inspiration.

Howard Brinton describes the meaning of the group in Quaker practice as follows: Light from God streams down to the waiting group; if way is open for this Light, it produces three results—unity, knowledge and power—which in turn produce the kind of behavior which exists as an ideal in a meeting for worship and a meeting for business. Because of the characteristics of the Light of Christ, a Quaker meeting or

8

organization inspired by Quakerism ought to evidence both a kind of relationship between people and a behavior in life expressive of the four qualities Community, Harmony, Equality and Simplicity.[4]

Such a meeting creates and exemplifies "the sort of behavior which ought to prevail everywhere." It is a laboratory and a training ground for the desired social order. "It may even become a germ cell of the new society of tomorrow."[5] Institutions and organizations growing out of such a milieu exist to serve the Kingdom of God in practical ways. They seek to give sustained expression, in both the ends they pursue and the means they employ, to Quakers' understanding of God's leading in concrete historical situations and, in the first instance, they are organized to serve very precise callings: to relieve the poor, to educate children, to aid victims of war and social injustice, to encourage beneficial legislation.

Our institutions are human attempts to meet human needs, under obedience to God. Though we believe that all of life can be sacramental, we do not regard the patterns in which we organize our lives as sacrosanct and unchangeable. Quakerism is perfectionist in its theology, but it has not created its organizations to serve, or to be served by, the already-perfected. Because our institutions are human creations they are also expressions of human error and frailty. They are the lengthened shadow of particular women and men, but they are also more than that. They are forms into which we pour our resources and our energy, our insights and our convictions. They are means of outreach beyond the limits of the Society of Friends and places where people of like conviction can gather. They are sources of strength, fellowship, and confirmation of our worth. They are laboratories for the desired social order. They are also, inevitably, channels for the expression of leadership, authority and power.

Because Quakers have renounced violence as an appropriate way to change people, each of the institutions we create must be, whatever its ends, committed to the means of persuasion or education. Community, Harmony, Equality and Simplicity can only be recommended by example. The ends of a particular Quaker organization may be to bring about rapid and radical political, social and economic change, but its means must acknowledge human beings as origins and ends in themselves and be organized to encourage growth in groups and individuals, even if that can only occur slowly. Ends and means must be congruent, though frequently in tension.

Here we recognize a crucial fact about our institutions: they can find the congruence between ends and means only by working through tension, conflict and compromise. Openness and flexibility do not occur free of anxiety and struggle. Organizations intended to exemplify Community, Harmony, Equality and Simplicity in their workings must develop social devices to use conflict effectively. Shaped and focused well, it becomes power, but it cannot merely be *managed*. Compromise must be the product of dynamism and growth, not blandness. Reconciliation must increase the power available, not divide it against itself. Such a social device for focusing the energy inherent in conflict, compromise, and reconciliation, on which all Quaker organizations more or less rely, is the Quaker business method, which depends on what Howard Brinton calls "agreeing upward."

Roger Wilson has written, "The sovereignty of God is understood to mean something for daily living. That sounds well, but only those who have ever borne administrative responsibility in an executive organization of Quaker consciences can have any idea how difficult it is to find the Will of God with enough constancy and confidence to provide administrative clarity."[6] A Friend who has lived a number of years in experimental religious communities once said that he was never able to see that there was a way of determining what color the Holy Spirit wanted the community to paint the kitchen walls. If the issue comes up—and it or something like it always will—we either spend time fruitlessly asking for divine guidance on a matter essentially neutral in its meaning for the spiritual life, or we let those with strong feelings decide the matter, or—at the worst—if we have people with strong opposing views on the subject—we paint the walls half one color, half the other.

Conflicts arise between the leadings or wishes of individuals and those of the group, between the accepted ways and new insights, between prophetic vision and institutional stability. Conflicts arise out of differences in degree of commitment to Quaker ideals or differences in emphasis on those ideals. They arise out of injured pride or personal antipathy which get dressed up as conflicts of conscience.

There are also conflicts, or at least strong tensions among the several ends of complex organizations, not only in setting priorities but also in deciding the balance between looking outward and looking inward. Community and Equality are both ends of Quaker organizations, but they often conflict with one another. Harmony, by which Howard Brinton means peacemaking, is a high value, but is it the pearl of great price, for which all other values must be sacrificed? Simplicity, which often expresses itself in blunt speaking, may threaten Harmony. The primary aims for which an organization has been created—to educate children, for example—may be in some tension with the end of Community when the question arises whether to retain someone who is a poor teacher but a fine person. The organization must then balance the accomplishment of its practical tasks with its need to treat its members, employees and participants humanely. Is it better, in such a case, to require the poor teacher to leave or to keep him on and serve the students less well? How shall such decisions be made? By debating the teacher's competence in public, or by letting a committee or headmaster make the determination? Quaker organizations must be self-reflective in order to learn how to "incorporate the spirit of compassion into the structure of an institution," as John Reader puts it,[7] but they cannot merely be turned in on themselves.

"To build humanity and charity into the life of an institution"[8] is to assert leadership. It is to find ways by which conflict can be transformed into focused energy and power. We cannot have the spirit of compassion incorporated into our structures, without effective leadership.

IV

Quaker institutions operate under the weight of great possibilities today. In a society experiencing a "twilight of authority," where every form of organization is threatening to break apart under the strain of its own contradictions and inadequacies, the need is desperate for "alternative structures." Quaker institutions are prominent among such "alternatives." But they have made their contribution to the search for new forms of authority at a very high cost. Our institutions have been going through a profound crisis of authority, which has expressed itself in great part as an incapacity to find or support leadership. In meetings, schools, colleges, national and international organizations we hear the same complaints. We cannot find enough effective leaders to meet our needs. Strong people are exhausted and broken by the demands of serving us. Vigorous, far-sighted people give up positions of responsibility, often out of frustration and resentment. They retreat to privatism to save their souls. Some of them become as cynical about the possibilities of maintaining effective Quaker institutions as the other members of those institutions feel about them. Either no one will take the positions available, or those who are willing to try to do the jobs are unseasoned and get little chance to grow in their work.

An invitation to serve a Quaker school as head or clerk, to serve a Quaker college as president, or to serve a Quaker board as executive director or secretary seems increasingly like an invitation to waste one's substance and break one's heart in dedication to illusory Quaker ideas of participation in and responsibility for decision-making.

That may seem an overstatement of the leadership problem facing Friends now and in the future, but I believe there are a number of sensitive, mature people who have given much of their lives to serving the Society who would attest to it as a description of their experience.

How do Quakers deal with issues of authority and power? Consider how we use a very familiar Quaker phrase, "Speak Truth to Power." Since the publication of the American Friends Service Committee's pamphlet with that title, in the 1950's, the phrase has become one of our great rallying cries. If we were to do a survey of phrases which seem to encapsulate liberal Quaker attitudes, I believe two phrases would head the list: "speak to that of God in everyone," which symbolizes our faith in the redeemability of the individual, and "speak truth to power," which symbolizes our despair of institutions.

"Speak truth to power" is a powerful exhortation, but like many powerful phrases, it has become overused. It has become a cliché we use to take the place of thought. Especially as a cliché the phrase deserves examination, for imbedded in it is much of our confusion and ambivalence about institutions, authority, leadership and power.

Let me recall the origin of the phrase. According to Steve Cary, the phrase just came to Milton Mayer one day, as he was thinking about the pamphlet. Everyone on the drafting committee liked it and asked where it came from. Milton Mayer thought he recalled it from some early Quaker writing, but no one subsequently found it, though Henry Cadbury made several attempts to find the phrase. In short, it would seem to have been original with Milton Mayer, though in sound and attitude it feels like an authentic expression of early Quakerism. It has its meaning for us, in part, because it is so concentrated and vivid an expression of an attitude toward government and other institutionalized forms of power. Surely it was the perfect title for a pamphlet challenging the behavior of the two antagonists of the Cold War. They represented raw, terrifying, unreflective and deadly power. What was called for to transform that power was bold and uncompromising truth.

The best way to understand the world situation then seemed to be in just such essentially allegorical terms. That is, Power, with a capital P, stood in opposition to Truth, also capitalized. And, as in all allegories, subtle distinctions were sacrificed for emotional impact. If your allegory needs someone called *Valiant for Truth,* his opponent will never be called *Valiant for Power.* In allegories we have no trouble telling the hero from the villain. There is no mistaking Mr. Worldly Wiseman for Christian.

Psychologically we continue to live in the starkly-defined allegorical world where Truth and Power are eternally antagonists. Neither the tactics we employ to challenge institutionalized power, nor the way we customarily talk about institutions suggests that we believe Truth and Power can ever genuinely come together. They are locked in a life and death battle. And when your opponent represents no truth, only power, all tactics appear to be acceptable.

What I believe we are experiencing is a distrust of power so deep that the institutions which we have created to act as channels for our religious concerns frequently find themselves paralyzed and incapable of any action, because to act is to exert power. This ambivalence toward the exercise of power appears very early in our history. The withdrawal of Friends from the government of Pennsylvania in 1756 is a good example. The choice facing Friends then was to maintain the peace testimony for the entire commonwealth, in the face of hostilities with the Indians, or to compromise their principles by supporting a build-up of military preparedness. Exercising responsible political power to protect the non-pacifist segments of the population seemed inconsistent with obeying the teachings of faith. So Friends decided to give up political power, and become, in effect, a Quaker party. This was an act of remarkable fidelity to principle, but three things should be said about it: First, the action was essentially an assertion that obedience to truth and obedience to the imperatives of political power are inimical to one another. Second, though Friends withdrew from bearing direct responsibility for power, they continued to bring a variety of influences, including the influence of the vote, to bear on legislatures and executives. That is, they were willing to wield a lot of power without ultimate responsibility. Third, this withdrawal from power in order to maintain a witness seems to be a confirmation of what Reinhold Niebuhr called the *irrelevance* of our pacifist ethic.

What was true in 1756 seems to be true today. We resist ultimate responsibility for actions, because that would be to acknowledge that we have power; we prefer to exert influence rather than power; and we would prefer to be irrelevant rather than ultimately accountable for our institutions' policies and actions.

We have passed through some fifteen years in which our ambivalence toward the exercise of power has led to two kinds of destructive reaction. At one extreme we have seen mindless rebellion which attacks the legitimacy of every action, defines every disputed decision as brutal oppression, and denies the humanity of whoever has authority or responsibility. At the other extreme we have seen people with very great power, authority or influence lose all courage of conviction in the face of these assaults and try to avoid the pains of responsibility by pretending they are in fact powerless.

In both cases we have seen the strong using, and claiming the right to use, the weapons of the helpless—passivity, un-cooperation, division and disruption, manipulation to block action, backbiting—to neutralize and dehumanize the opponent.

Both kinds of reaction exemplify what Sartre called "bad faith," which he defines as pretending we are the helpless victims of circumstance instead of taking responsibility for our choices and our actions. New, more humane forms of authority are needed in our society, but certain Quaker ways of responding to responsibility will not help us to find them.

Let me illustrate how bad faith is practiced. In 1967 Jerry Farber first published his essay "The Student as Nigger." Hundreds of thousands read it, especially younger people. The essay argued that the subordinate position students found themselves in, in schools and colleges, could be best understood as analogous to the position Black people had held under slavery. "Students are niggers. When you get that straight, our schools begin to make sense." Students were politically disenfranchised; they had little or no influence over what the curriculum offered or demanded. In some schools, restrooms and dining rooms were separate for faculty and students, as another symbol of the master-slave relationship which obtained between them. Students were being deliberately and systematically denied equality and humanity. They were "niggers."

Farber's essay successfully shocked many people into reflecting on power issues; it helped some students realize that they could take more responsibility for their education, and it led some teachers and administrators into examining—and in some cases changing—patterns of governance. Nonetheless, the essay stands, I believe, as a striking example of bad faith, for not only was its analogy fundamentally false but its way of pressing that analogy helped justify people in their evasion of responsibility. This false analogy let one of the most powerful, influential segments of American society deny its enormous economic, political, and social power. One need not dispute the validity of Farber's criticism of institutional insensitivity and violence toward young people to say that for affluent, white, middle-class American college students to claim that they were "the new niggers" was to demonstrate an outrageous self-centeredness and profound insensitivity to what being a "nigger" has meant in America. But the analogy was very inviting because it let so many people appropriate the suffering of others and claim it for themselves. Soon a great many other segments of the society were claiming the same title. It was convenient for faculty, then administrators, then government employees and similar power centers to claim support and sympathy by insisting that, since they were treated badly and not consulted about their own futures, *they* were "the new niggers." And while white middle-class groups squabbled over who was the most down-trodden and oppressed, the truly oppressed were once more ignored or thrust out of the way. Worse, the oppression which Blacks, Chicanos and poor Whites experienced was minimized or trivialized by the *powerful,* who appropriated their experience for the most self-serving of reasons. "You can't hold me to account for what I do, or the position I hold; I am as oppressed as you are."

Farber's essay gave us a slogan for an attitude. The slogan may no longer have the same currency, but the attitude is still very much with us. It is the attitude that reduces the complexity of authority relationships to the single one of slave and master. Notice the implications of such attitudes as are captured by such phrases as "the student as nigger" and "speak Truth to Power" for our work in our Quaker institutions. Precisely those Friends who insist on the importance of openness and flexibility in the search for truth in every other situation find themselves becoming absolutist about their truth-claims as soon as they can identify an institution or a representative of the authority of an institution—a clerk or executive secretary, teacher, administrator, board member—as the opponent. Then all flexibility and subtlety of understanding characteristic of these Friends in other circumstances tend to disappear. We deny the holder of power his humanity by picturing him as slavemaster or absolute tyrant, but we say it is the *power* itself which dehumanized him. We put him outside our fellowship, in the name of Community. It is as though the only working definition of *power* is *error* or *evil*, and the truth is clear and unambiguous.

V

Let me offer a parable of our situation. Several years ago I was teaching Thoreau's *Walden* in a freshman humanities class. One day the discussion veered off from the text to an argument about individualism, institutions, and power. Several of my students argued that there was not enough support for individualism in American society; a few others argued that some of our most important institutions were being damaged because the excesses of individualism were so great and so unchecked. Inevitably the discussion shifted to whether institutions like colleges did not exert too much power over students and thus destroy their individualism.

After a time, to focus on the problems of authority and power, I threw my book into the middle of the room and asked

17

my students to imagine that it represented the power to do whatever one wanted with the college. All anyone would have to do would be to pick up the book, in order to have power to affect whatever he or she wanted. How the power was to be used would depend on the ethical standards of whoever picked up the book. My students were rather sobered at the prospect I was offering them, and for a time no one moved. Then an older student—a former career navy man now a pacifist—tentatively made a motion to stand up. Immediately another student, who had insisted that there was not enough support for individualism in American society, leaped from his chair, rushed to the center of the class, *and stood on the book!*

Let me emphasize the point. My student was deeply suspicious of the exercise of power. He would not, therefore, pick up the book and acknowledge that he was willing to be treated with as one with authority. He was not willing to stand for what he believed in, but he would prevent everyone else from acting on their beliefs. He would not act affirmatively, but he would block any action. He would deny his use of power in the very act of preventing anyone else from using it.

So much for bad faith. Now for denial and evasion.

Because we are so fearful of power, in our institutions we try to deny that anyone has it, or we insist that everyone but us has more influence over events. Moreover, we hedge authority around with impossible conditions, as though to assure that it will be exercised clumsily. We hold our presidents, heads of schools or secretaries responsible for what happens to the organizations they administer, but boards, committees and constituents do everything they can to neutralize those leaders' ability to act, while evading responsibility themselves for unpopular decisions. Action is the exercise of power, and power is oppression. The newest student, the least seasoned staff member, the least sensitive committee member can exercise influence out of all proportion to his ability or experience simply by attacking the legitimacy of any action he disapproves of, or by insisting that he has not been listened to because he has failed to convince others to agree with him, or by complaining that he feels oppressed and treated like a slave.

I have known some students who thought they had the right to deny the *legitimacy* of decisions made half a dozen years before they had even applied to the College. I do not mean that they objected that the decisions were mistaken and therefore ought to be reconsidered; that is always appropriate, even when it is inconvenient. No, having discovered that they could not persuade people that the decisions were mistaken, they argued that the decisions had no standing because *they* had not been part of the consultative process. To persist in acting on such decisions, therefore, would violate the sense of community. It would be an act of oppression against those who had not been consulted. I have known some faculty members, and more than a few parents and Quaker constituents of the College, who thought we would be oppressive if we did not reconsider such decisions solely on that basis—as though Quaker business procedure required not only an absolute democracy but also behaving as though every day is the First Day of Creation.

I have heard students say that they were oppressed by the very fact that a course had a pre-arranged reading list, or by the requirement in a course to write papers or to follow standard English usage. During the worst of these past years, the competence of the teacher, as expressed through booklists and assignments, became for the most alienated of our students an assertion of force over them.

I have also known teachers so determined not to be authoritative that they lost all capacity to give direction or leading to people who needed it. We have seen teachers desperate to be mistaken for students, aping their dress and speech and attitudes, making up whole reading lists from last year's underground books, or refusing to create any booklists, assignments or even the minimal class structure, because to do any of that was to enslave students. And what was happening in schools and colleges was also happening, in other ways, in other kinds of Quaker institutions.

Nor are boards and committees of control willing to bear the burden of leadership. How often a president, head, or executive secretary is given a specific charge by the board—reduce the budget, remove an ineffective staff member, re-establish firm discipline—only to find, when the policy directive causes objections, that the promised board support has melted like snow flurries in May. Suddenly the board, which has been very clear that *it* determined policy, presents itself as only advisory to this clumsy, insensitive administrator. One board member after another says something like, ''I never really felt easy with what the board was saying,'' or ''it's true the board told you to act, but some of us now are having second thoughts,'' or ''we told you we wanted action, but we didn't mean for you to be so precipitant'' or finally, ''Well, we hadn't realized your action would make so many people unhappy.''

Many of us have heard such comments, if indeed we haven't made them. Evasion and denial of responsibility start with the pronouns: under pressure *we* becomes *they* or *you* or *it*. ''*The board* certainly told *you* to proceed, but *we* are having second thoughts.''

That sort of undermining of leaders is neither new nor peculiar to Friends. I suggest, however, that in our current situation we undermine our leaders with great frequency, and with terrible effect on them and on our institutions, in large part because we do not want to be *the establishment*, even in the institutions we have established. Too much of our pride is wrapped up in picturing ourselves as daring rebels, iconoclasts, challengers of the system or establishment.

Many times in the past twenty years I have found myself fondly thinking how much more comfortable it would be to teach in a large non-Quaker university. *Then* I could speak Truth to Power. I would not have to take responsibility for this machine called the university; instead I could be its most powerful and righteous critic. Anything I could do to humanize it even slightly would be counted in my favor. I could be a constant thorn in the flesh to the administration, and I could probably even count on being protected as an endangered species, a pet Quaker. I could be independent at the small price of being powerless and irrelevant. I am not claiming that this is a fair description of what it is like to be a Quaker in a big university. Much of my reason for writing this essay is to make better distinctions between reality and fantasy. In acknowledging my fantasy, however, I believe I describe something characteristic in many Friends' attitudes today. We do not want to be the establishment: we want always to be the rebel, the champion of the underdog. We prefer to perceive ourselves, and to be perceived, as alienated from authority and power.

Virtually everyone in a Quaker institution wants to be outside the sphere of responsibility, *but well inside the sphere of influence*. We want to be able to dance at everyone's wedding. So we fall back on the false allegory. We want to champion Community in opposition to the institution; we want to stand for Equality in opposition to authority. We want to be the ones to speak Truth to that convenient abstraction, Power.

A Pendle Hill annual report from the mid-nineteen-seventies says "we cannot afford to relearn the meaning and structure of Pendle Hill every year." That sentence speaks volumes about our difficulty in living with the fact of authority and power. In one sense we must relearn the meaning and structure of any institution every year, but in the past we have done so by taking previous experience, history, and tradition as one valid means to learn. "New occasions teach new duties," but we have to know and respect our own past experience enough to be able to discern when we are, in fact, confronting a new occasion, and when the appropriate response to that occasion is a re-affirmation of a long-held conviction. It is infinitely harder to *relearn* something if we begin by rejecting any validity for tradition or previous experience. It is essential to reconsider past decisions to determine whether they are still wise and just, but our institutions cannot survive as channels for the expression of our religious convictions if every feeling of disgruntlement is to be taken seriously as a challenge to the *right* of everyone to have made *any* decision in the past. That someone feels oppressed is a cause for concern, but it may be best dealt with by helping the individual recognize that his feelings are not necessarily an accurate description of objective reality.

Sometimes an individual has to get over, or outgrow, offended feelings.

Bad faith flourishes where false analogies, false allegories, and abstractions are used to avoid facing concrete realities. Let me offer an example. I was visiting Pendle Hill during a time of considerable turmoil in the student body and staff. Two old friends, in particular, wanted to talk to me at great length about the insensitivity and oppressive behavior of "the administration." I am used to that phrase for talking about the federal government and large universities; I can even see reasons for using it to talk about how a small college is run. But, as I told my friends, "What you are calling *the administration* is two people. You have known them by their first names for many years; you eat two meals a day with them, perhaps wash dishes with them, worship with them every day. No matter how troubled you are by their actions, what do you gain in clarity of meaning by speaking of *the administration* of Pendle Hill, instead of talking about X and Y?"

My friends did not have much of an answer. Indeed, they didn't pay much attention to the question. Theirs was a battle on the highest plane of principle. They represented Truth, and X and Y—who had first names, ate meals in the dining room and washed dishes in the kitchen, and who, moreover, felt pain when attacked, like the rest of us—represented Power. My two old friends were *we*, X and Y were *they*. And it is better not to think too much about how *they* hurt, for then *we* must reflect on the weapons *we* use against *them*. X and Y must be made into abstractions—which is to say de-humanized—because only thinking in abstractions—or allegorical figures—will allow us to wage battle in a total fashion.

In her recent history, *Pendle Hill: A Quaker Experiment*, Eleanore Price Mather says of Pendle Hill's change in pattern of governance, that shifting from a directorship to a system of five departments and an executive clerk eased the strain on the individual in that position and "also removed the image of personal dominance which provoked resentment in many students." That phrase is worth lingering over. Did the director actually dominate Pendle Hill in the recent past? What Eleanore Mather's history tells us is that, when the Board named an acting director and directors of studies, the appointments were challenged by the resident community, students, and staff. But neither then, nor during the tenure of the last people to be given the title "director," is there much evidence that the directors dominated life at Pendle Hill. Instead, what is shown is an increasing polarization between "administration and anti-administration sympathies, . . . pro-administration forces regarding Pendle Hill as an educational institution, opposing forces seeing it as a community—or possibly as a commune, which it definitely was not."[9]

The very title, *director,* carries official authority, by virtue of which the holder of the office represents the weight of tradition, the weight of an institution's ideals and purposes. It represents structure, a board of managers charged with final decision-making for the school. The title suggests that somebody, before the beginning of a school year, has reflected on where the institution might be going that year. It suggests that someone has been delegated the authority to *direct* a school in some directions, not in others, and certainly not in *every* direction. It is significant, I believe, that "the image of personal dominance" is what provoked resentment; the "image," the symbol of authority is enough to provoke resentment in some people.

The nature of the allegory—in which pure Truth confronts raw Power, in which there are only two characters, Slave and Master—requires that any director, any person in authority, be challenged as an instrument of oppression. Nothing and no one shall have more weight than I: not the historic aims of the school, not the weight of long-time seasoned leaders, not the weight of previous experience and service. Why should we assume that a long-seasoned Quaker leader knows more about how to live in community than an earnest college drop-out who has been "turned-off" by formal education? They are equal in the sight of God, so why should one have more authority for the running of Pendle Hill than the other? If one of them is *given* the authority of a title and responsibility, that can only be understood as an application of raw force, and must be resented accordingly.

A style of anti-leader has arisen among Friends, one who despises all compromise, who blocks any group action until he gets his way, who makes the leading of his conscience the final arbiter for the rightness of the group's action, and who practices a rhetoric of inarticulate earnestness to assert his moral superiority over all established institutions.

VI

In his first letter to the Corinthians St. Paul develops the metaphor of the church as the body of Christ. Though there are many parts, each has its own functions and each is worthy of respect for what it contributes to the whole and for being part of the whole. "There are varieties of gifts, but the same spirit. There are varieties of service, but the same Lord. There are many forms of work, but all of them, in all men, are the work of the same God. In each of us the Spirit is manifested in one particular way, for some useful purpose." (I Cor. 12: 4-8.)

This is the outline of a system of leadership within the Christian community, where all are equal in the eyes of God, but each has different gifts. Such a system of leadership tries to balance "the tension between the moral equality which is basic to freedom and the hierarchy which is basic to orderly and dependable social organization."[10]

This church government of the primitive church was the model early Friends sought to follow. They recognized gifts of leadership—as in the recording of ministers and naming of elders, overseers and clerks—but they made the whole community of faith the final interpreter of God's leadings, in the meeting for worship and for business. They knew gifts could be abused—the earliest days are full of terrible examples—but they also knew gifts could be nurtured, strengthened, and focused. They did not, therefore, treat gifts in leadership as dangers to be checked or restrained. Instead, they confirmed people in their skills; they encouraged them to develop; as new people came into the community of faith, they were encour-

24

aged and educated into appropriate use of their gifts. Always there is the reference back from the individual leading to the group's leading, so that an individual's leading can be confirmed and supported by the meeting, but equally so that the meeting can be gathered and strengthened by obedience to the leading brought to it by an individual.

This system, evolved by three centuries of Quakerism, does not eliminate tension. At its best it uses the energy in that tension so that the resolution which comes from "agreeing upward" has greater power. At its worst, however, it dissipates energy and power, paralyzes action, and achieves only the blandest of resolutions.

To outline this Quaker pattern of governance is to realize how changed our circumstances are today. In the seventeenth century the Quaker "community of faith" was unquestionably Christian in its beliefs, and this agreement on belief was further reinforced as meetings became highly homogeneous in membership. "The world's people" had little contact with or influence on Quaker organizations. It would be foolish to mourn the passing of those days; the vitality of Quaker-inspired institutions today is the result of reaching out beyond the homogeneous meeting and drawing in, as full participants, people of other traditions or persuasions. Control of Quaker schools, colleges, the American Friends Service Committee and other groups no longer rests absolutely with the parent body of organizational Quakerism. If we want to use the Quaker system of leadership today, we must do so with full awareness of our different situation.

In recent years, much attention has been given to democratizing our institutions by broadening representation on boards and by drawing more people into decision-making. That is clearly in the spirit of Quakerism and ought to be encouraged in the future. But much of the argument for greater participation in decision-making has been framed as an attack on the very notion of leaders and leadership. In several cases, governance has been restructured to get away from the pattern of a director or president as a *dominant* leader. Thomas S. Brown's pamphlet, *Friends as Leaders,* warns against leaders being wielders of power.

> We should not affirm leaders solely because of human qualities often associated with leadership. For example, winsomeness and forcefulness of personality, articulateness, the ability to organize and to inspire, intellectual capacity, helpful as these are, are yet insufficient standards. Without divine guidance in our selection, we may appoint inauthentic leadership which easily becomes self-serving or ineffective.[11]

This is a good warning, but it expresses more fear than hope. The list of "human qualities often associated with leadership" makes them seem like a minefield of dangers. As is so often the case when we speak of leadership, we think in *either-or* rather than *both-and* terms. The issue in finding and nurturing leaders is not to suppress gifts but to give full respect to those already evident while considering what gifts will need further maturing.

There are many kinds and many sources of authority, none of which is necessarily to be disparaged in itself. One may have personal gifts of eloquence and clarity of insight which earn the respect of colleagues. This is authority conferred by general agreement. One may have professional competence or expertise, confirmed by standing in a "guild." One may have organizational competence, a sense of how to get people to work together, or political influence with colleagues and other decision-makers. This is authority earned by the results of one's previous work. One may have great congruence with an institution or community, which confers the authority to speak for it. Authority may also come from *ex officio* position—conferred by trustees or a board—or by tradition or custom, which confers authority on senior people, for example.

In a Quaker institution, several of these kinds of authority may come together to make up what is called "weight." The weighty Friend may express the community's best mind, or understand how best to get something done. The person who has borne responsibility for a long time, or whose official position brings access to a lot of information, may also speak or act with ''weight.''

Of course the greatest authority comes from the Holy Spirit, which leads one to know, communicate and act on the Truth. Discerning that authority can be difficult, however; even the most faithful person will struggle with doubts about the validity of a leading. Simply lacking other kinds of authority is not in itself very good evidence that one has the authority of the Spirit.

Effective leadership comes from the marriage of vision with practical skills of organization and personal eloquence; respect for persons and responsibility for the group with the ability to assess the consequences of actions; decisiveness with patience; the capacity to take satisfaction in the accomplishment of others with the willingness to be held accountable for one's decisions and actions. It is the rare person who has most of those qualities in the ideal proportions. But these and other human qualities can be developed. They all rest on skills to be learned, but skills are developed by practice, and people practice skills only if the results justify the effort. The beginning musician has to feel an increase in control over the instrument and more pleasure in the resulting sounds. The new teacher has to feel that the energy expended on a class is being replenished by the response of the students.

Abraham Maslow has a schematic representation of human growth which shows the person in the middle, pulled in opposite directions by the demand for safety, on the one hand, and the demand for growth, on the other. Every movement toward growth, in other words, is taken at the cost of some degree of safety. People can move toward growth if the loss of safety can be minimized or the promise of growth can be maximized.

We all learn best when we are supported by others' encouragement. So it is with leadership skills; there have to be rewards for practicing them; the energy they require must come back to the individual as increased satisfaction, the sense of a job well done, people helped, valuable purposes accomplished. Through such rewards, the Spirit works; it nurtures us in leadership by humanizing us, it frees us to be compassionate by letting us feel the compassion and support of others. Skills develop where they are valued and respected. Where there is no compassion or support, only suspicion and contempt, there will be no growth in leadership.

Friends as Leaders stresses developing leaders who are servant-leaders rather than wielders of power. Such a model for leadership offers us a great deal, but it must give us a more sophisticated examination of the nature of power before it can adequately meet our needs. Here is the *either-or* error, again. Leadership is not a matter of being a servant *or* wielding power; it is learning to wield power *as* a servant. Leaders must inevitably wield some power or see it wielded by someone else, perhaps someone without any responsibility for its effects. A sober knowledge of power—like a respectful knowledge of electricity—can lead to its effective and appropriate use. Power wielded evasively or in bad faith is already corrupted.

In the life of the Society of Friends we need many kinds of leadership. We need planners and organizers, gatherers of resources, directors of projects, people who can speak on our behalf, clerks who can draw a group together to produce consensus. We also need the kinds of leaders Wolf Mendl has distinguished as the visionaries and the realists, or the prophets and the reconcilers. "A 'visionary' or 'prophet' . . . is filled by a vision of the ideal and attentive to its fulfillment . . . a 'realist' or 'reconciler' [has] his attention . . . focused on concrete particulars . . . "[12] And as we need many kinds of leadership, we also need the tension produced by such a multiplicity of visions and goals.

The clerk of a business meeting is pre-eminently a leader as servant. The job requires the fullest measure of self-denial. The good clerk uses his or her skills to discern where the group is prepared to go and to reflect back to the group what agreement it is reaching.

When I was clerk of the Earlham faculty, I described the job of presiding over faculty meeting as like taking eighty kangaroos for a walk. Discovering where a lot of kangaroos want to go and informing them of the direction they are taking is no small task, but neither is it very great leadership, for ultimately the clerk is impotent to influence action.

It is an extremely important kind of leadership, but it is only one kind, and by itself it cannot be enough to give force and direction to the work of the Society. But because we are so fearful of the exercise of power, we have tended to make the clerk the only acceptable model for Quaker leadership. Presidents, heads, and directors disappear; in their place we find clerks. To the extent that such changes are merely cosmetic, they both confirm our fear of the exercise of power and exacerbate our difficulties. To the extent that all other expressions of leadership get swallowed up by that single model, we are evading the full responsibilities of power by choosing only the blandest form of leadership.

A clerk cannot be the servant-leader, if everyone else is a freelance, following his own lead or preference. The clerk then is merely a figurehead, presiding over the collapse of meaningful community. The servant-leader can be effective only where the principle of leading by serving is knit into the whole fabric of the institution. Everyone who is part of the community must accept the principle in his or her own life; it must be the basis for the novitiate-period of anyone coming into the institution. If we do not express that ideal at every level of institutional life, it will serve only to paralyze our leaders further. For there are as serious dangers in the servant-leader model as there are in any other. If the servant-leader operates in the old dominance-submission framework, where if I win someone else must lose, the servant will become simply the perfect bureaucrat. "Don't blame me, I only take orders." Where fear for safety is great, growth is small. Recent Quaker institutional history has shown us that leaders who have tried to be servants have frequently been oppressed by a great many imperious, irresponsible, and capricious would-be masters.

The servant-leader must *lead,* which means to set goals and directions, to channel energy, to persuade and organize: to wield power, in short. This is to show what David McClelland has called "the positive face of power" which, he says, is characterized by a concern for finding the group goals which will move people, for helping them formulate these goals, for taking initiative in giving group members the means to achieve those goals, and for giving them "the feeling of strength and competence they need to work for such goals" "The ultimate paradox of social leadership and social power," according to David McClelland, is that "to be an effective leader, one must turn all of his so-called followers into leaders."[13]

Identifying and formulating goals can be achieved by a clerk, but giving people the means, and encouragement to work for goals, are tasks beyond the role of the clerk. They are enabling ministry or service which rests, in part, on transmitting enthusiasm and energy and translating them into power. Such a leader is a kind of educator, helping to set goals, as opposed to merely recording them, communicating the goals wisely, through the gifts of eloquence and persuasion, taking initiatives to formulate means to achieve the goals, by gathering and organizing resources, and inspiring the group to work for its goals, by persuasion and by personal example.

The servant-leader serves only one master, the truth which is from God. That truth is sometimes very clear, but more often it is only tentatively known. The servants of truth must search for it diligently and stand under its authority. We try to test the genuineness of leadings by their fruits: Do they draw together the community of faith and give it more power? Do they bring greater harmony and justice into the life of the community or institution? Do they put the needs of the weakest in the fellowship first? Do they address issues clearly, accurately and sensitively? These are not absolute tests of a leading, but they point in the right directions. In these years of anti-authoritarianism, however, the tendency has been to judge a leading's authenticity by very different standards: Does the leading challenge existing institutions? Does it reduce the influence or power of established leaders or organizations? But not all who cry "Lord, Lord" or who speak of "the community" or who claim to speak truth to power have submitted themselves to the mastery of truth.

I have suggested we have been living in a false allegory. In a true allegory, everything which we see acted out in symbolic form in the outer world reflects the experience within each human soul, so we gain self-knowledge. Truth struggles with falsehood in the world out there, but also within my soul. Truth confronts power in the political world, and in the inner world of each human being. In a false allegory we project on others the fears, anxieties, and angers which can only be comprehended, resolved, and turned into strengths when we acknowledge that they originate within ourselves. Our dealing with our institutions and our leaders has been largely that kind of projection, and we have consequently remained without self-knowledge. The fears, anxieties, and angers remain in us, festering and enfeebling us. We dehumanize others and in the process dehumanize ourselves. Power and truth must meet and be reconciled within our hearts as well as within our institutions.

Let us acknowledge that American society is still in the midst of hard times. People have been savaged by institutions, even by Quaker institutions. But not all the injury has been done to the student, the young person, or the junior staff person. We have also seen gifted, sensitive leaders driven out of callings which made use of their gifts by the aggression and hostility of people incapable of living within the constraints of community. In rejecting the idols of power and organization, we turned to another set of idols—those of unreflective individualism, hedonism, and self-centeredness. We have to learn to be free of both sets of idols.

We are seeing the collapse and paralysis of many traditional institutions. In their place may arise better alternatives, and here Friends may have a contribution to make. But it is equally possible that we will see more authoritarian, less humane institutions and organizations come to dominate this society. If we want to throw our weight behind the first alternative, we must address the problem of developing and sustaining new leadership in the Religious Society of Friends. But that cannot be separated from re-examining, reforming, developing, and sustaining vital institutions to serve us. We must try to get new bearings. We have before us the work of reconciliation between the needs of individuals and the needs of social institutions—which may also be the expression of community among worshippers and students and activitists. We also have to learn more about the social history of our institutions, to bring objective, sympathetic analysis to bear on their strengths and weaknesses. To understand our institutions, and therefore to understand more about ourselves as individuals, we must clear our minds of cant—the slogans and clichés which substitute for clear thought—and stop living in bad faith.

In his Swarthmore Lecture, *Of Schools and Schoolmasters,* John Reader says "It is comparatively easy to show understanding and love if we are not in a position of authority; it is a challenge that exists in any age to build humanity and charity into the life of an institution and to reconcile the function of government with the exercise of love and friendship."[14]

Meeting the challenge Reader describes is the great work ahead of us. The failures of the past, if we will face them honestly, can give us bearings by which we navigate the future.

FOOTNOTES

[1]Nisbet, Robert, Preface, *The Twilight of Authority* (New York: Oxford University Press, 1975).

[2]Wood, H. E., Introduction, p.vii, in Lloyd, Arnold, *Quaker Social History: 1669–1738* (London: Longmans, Green, 1950).

[3]Lloyd, p. 1.

[4]Brinton, Howard, *Friends for 300 Years* (Wallingford, Pa.: Pendle Hill, 1965), p.119.

[5]Brinton, Howard, *Quaker Education in Theory and Practice* (Wallingford, Pa.: Pendle Hill, 1940), pp.24–25.

[6]Wilson, Roger C., *Authority, Leadership and Concern*, Swarthmore Lecture 1949 (London: FHSC), p.57.

[7]Reader, John, *Of Schools and Schoolmasters*, Swarthmore Lecture 1979 (London: FHSC), p.66.

[8]Reader, p. 13.

[9]Mather, Eleanore Price, *Pendle Hill: A Quaker Experiment in Education and Community* (Wallingford, Pa.: Pendle Hill, 1980), p.98.

[10]Wilson, p. 76.

[11](Privately printed, 1979; distributed by Pendle Hill), p.10.

[12]Mendl, Wolf, *Prophets and Reconcilers*, Swarthmore Lecture 1974 (London: FHSC), p. 8.

[13]McClelland, David C., "The Two Faces of Power," *Journal of International Affairs,* XXIV, No.1 (1970), 40–41.

[14]Reader, p. 13.